The Soul Remembers

A Journey of Return Through Soul Memory, Divine Origin, and Eternal Knowing

blanche johanna

© 2025 blanche johanna

All rights reserved.

No part of this publication may be reproduced, stored in a retrieval system, or transmitted in any form or by any means, electronic, mechanical, photocopying, recording, or otherwise, without the prior written permission of the author.

This book is a spiritual and creative transmission intended to support personal and collective awakening. All guidance and reflections are shared from the author's lived and intuitive experience and are not intended as a substitute for professional advice.

The Soul Remembers™ is a trademark of blanche johanna. All rights reserved.

ISBN: 978-1-7641285-2-0

www.blanchejohanna.com

Dedication

To the ones who came before me
To the fragments I gathered with trembling hands
To the light I almost forgot
And to the soul who never left me

We are not here to become
we are here to remember

before the body
before the breath
before the beginning
there was light

not the kind that blinds, but the kind that knows
soft ancient light that cradled the soul
you were that light
not born into it
but formed of it

you chose to forget so you could remember
you chose separation so you could feel return
you scattered so you could gather
you broke open so you could shine through

each lifetime a thread
each ache a signal
each longing a map back to yourself
back to the whole
back to the truth that never left

there are no lost pieces
only sleeping ones
and now they stir

you have not missed the path
you are the path

you are the opening
you are the return

this is not a story
it is a remembering
and it has already begun

you are the memory rising
you are the flame that remained
you are the soul that remembers

Remembrance Map

The Cries of the Soul
Signs of the Remembering

The Veil of Forgetting
Entering the Human Dream

Ancestral Echoes
Inheriting What Was Never Ours

The Sacred Pause
Separation, Stillness & the Space Between

The Twin Flame Mirror
Love as a Catalyst for Awakening

Starseed Origins & Celestial Homes
Remembering Where We Come From

Soul Alchemy
Chaos, Purging & Integration

Embodiment
Becoming the Living Light

The Return
Wholeness, Remembrance & Homecoming

Chapter One

The Cries of the Soul: Signs of the Remembering

Restlessness, longing, dreams, synchronicities, early awakenings of a soul calling itself back into wholeness

It begins slowly
a restlessness you can't explain
a longing with no name
a hunger that no person
no job
no place
can satisfy

You try to soothe it with routine
with goals
with reason
but nothing lands
nothing holds

And in the quiet
the soul begins to speak
not in words
but in symbols
in dreams
in strange timings that feel like too much to be coincidence

You see the same numbers over and over
feel drawn to places you've never been
meet eyes with strangers who feel familiar
hear whispers in music
see yourself in poetry

You start to question everything
and yet somehow feel closer to truth than ever before

This is not confusion
this is remembering
in motion
fragment by fragment
light slipping through the cracks

The soul does not shout, it stirs
it nudges
it places mirrors where you once saw walls

You may not know what is happening
but something in you does

You are not going mad
you are going home

This is the ache before the awakening
the divine discomfort
the cry of the soul saying
I'm still here
come find me
we are not done yet

Integration

- What forms has my soul's restlessness taken over the years?

- Can I recall moments that felt like messages, signs, or quiet truths calling me deeper?

- How did I respond when the first cracks in the illusion began to appear?

- What part of me has always known, even when my mind couldn't explain it?

- What synchronicities have gently reminded me that I am being guided?

I honour the quiet ways my soul speaks
Through signs, through longing, through moments
that don't make sense but feel true
I no longer dismiss what I feel
I trust that something deeper is unfolding
And I open to the remembering that has already begun

Chapter Two

The Veil of Forgetting: Entering the Human Dream

The descent into form, the soul's agreement to forget, and the divine reason we chose to remember in fragments

Before you remembered
you agreed to forget

You were light without end
formless
whole
woven into the fabric of all that is

But there was a calling
not of pain
not of punishment
but of purpose

To enter the dream
to descend into form
to feel the ache of separation
so that love could be remembered
not as an idea
but as a lived return

You chose a body
You chose amnesia
You chose parents
You chose a path with forgetting stitched into its first breath
Because to remember would mean more
if it came through your own awakening

This veil was never punishment
It was sacred agreement
A divine forgetting
that allowed the soul to journey into experience
into contrast

into the illusion of other
only so it could one day find its way back

The pain was real
The confusion was deep
But underneath it all
a thread remained

A golden thread of knowing
tugging softly across timelines
through heartbreak
through silence
through longing
It whispered, there is more
You have not lost it
You are simply remembering in fragments

You came here not to escape the human
but to embody the divine through it
To bring light into the density
To anchor heaven through skin

This is the soul's journey
not to rise above
but to descend with awareness
To forget just enough
to make remembering sacred

You are not behind
You are not broken
You are right on time
And the veil
is thinning

Integration

- What does the veil of forgetting mean to me at this stage of my journey?

- In what ways have I experienced the ache of separation, and how has it shaped me?

- Can I sense the golden thread that has guided me, even in moments of darkness?

- What parts of me are beginning to stir, ready to be remembered?

- How does it feel to know I chose this path with purpose?

I trust that I came here with intention
Even in the forgetting, I was never truly lost
Each ache is a doorway, each moment a thread
I honour the path I chose, and I open to the
remembrance rising within me now

Chapter Three

Ancestral Echoes: Inheriting What Was Never Ours

How ancestral imprints, karmic debris, and cellular memory shape our path until we choose to transmute them

They were not your wounds
but they lived in you
They whispered through your blood
etched patterns into your choices
wove themselves into your nervous system
until you couldn't tell where they ended and you
began

The grief that didn't make sense
the fear that came from nowhere
the weight you carried without story
none of it began with you

You came into this life carrying the dust of
generations
unspoken trauma
unfinished songs
unshed tears folded into your DNA
because your soul said yes

Yes, I will be the one to remember
Yes, I will be the one to clear the debris
Yes, I will end what was never mine but lived in me
like it was

This was not burden
This was agreement
a sacred soul contract to transmute what could not
yet be freed

You were born into a lineage not to repeat it
but to rewrite it
to feel what they couldn't

to speak what they silenced
to forgive what they carried
and to lay it down

What was inherited can be healed
What was absorbed can be released
You do not have to carry what never belonged to you

You are not betraying your ancestors by letting go
You are liberating them
and yourself

This is the alchemy of remembrance
not to hold it all
but to honour it and then release it back to light

You are the soft ending of a hard story
the final echo dissolving into peace
the one who remembers differently

Integration

- What have I inherited that no longer feels like mine to carry?
- Where do I feel ancestral pain in my body or patterns?
- Can I sense the difference between what is mine and what is not?
- What would it mean to honour my lineage without being bound by it?
- Am I ready to release what has been held for generations?

I honour the story that brought me here
I see the pain that shaped the path, and I choose to set it down
With love and reverence, I release what no longer belongs to me
I walk forward free, with only light in my bones

Chapter Four

The Sacred Pause: Separation, Stillness & the Space Between

When connection is lost, paths diverge, or silence settles in, the space where the soul breathes, breaks, and begins again

There comes a time when everything goes quiet
The path splits
the phone doesn't ring
the messages stop
the one who stirred your soul is suddenly far

And you wonder if it was ever real

This is the sacred pause
the space between the soul's inhale and its return to breath
not punishment
not abandonment
but necessary stillness

You ache
you ache more than you thought possible
and still, there is no answer
no closure
just silence

But beneath that silence
a new current begins
one that doesn't rush
one that asks you to sit in the not-knowing
to listen to yourself when no one else can fill the void

The separation is not separation at all
it is spaciousness
a reorientation
a call to meet yourself as deeply as you once longed to be met

You learn to sit with the ache
to soften toward your own reflection
to stop waiting for the other
and start listening to the one within

This is where your light returns
not all at once
but in pieces
each one discovered in the stillness
each one placed back inside you like it never left

The space between was always part of the design
because in the pause
you find presence
and in the presence
you remember

Integration

- Where in my life have I experienced a sacred pause or unexpected stillness?
- How have I responded to silence or separation when it felt confusing or painful?
- Can I now see that space not as abandonment, but as soul invitation?
- What has emerged in me because of the quiet?
- How does it feel to honour the in-between as part of the journey?

I honour the pauses
The stillness
The spaces that once felt empty, but were filled
with unseen becoming
I no longer rush to fill the quiet
I listen
I soften
I receive what only silence can reveal

Chapter Five

The Twin Flame Mirror: Love as a Catalyst for Awakening

The divine meeting of counterparts that ignites remembrance, triggers purification, and returns us to the heart of truth

You see them
and something ancient unlocks
not just in your heart
but in your soul

It's not recognition
it's remembrance
a knowing so deep, it doesn't need explanation
only breath

The Twin Flame is not a partner
not a possession
not a reward for healing
they are your mirror
your equal
your echo across time

They awaken everything
the love
the ache
the divinity
the shadow

Not because they are trying to
but because your soul asked for it
because union cannot be built on illusion
and they have come to burn it all away

You will see yourself in them
the beauty
the resistance
the parts you denied
the light you abandoned

You will want to hold on
and you will want to run
you will feel home
and completely undone

But this is the sacred fire
the mirror that purifies through love
not gentle love
but truth-love
the kind that doesn't flinch
the kind that brings you back to yourself again and again

It is not always easy
but it is always exact
divine timing
divine alignment
divine remembrance

You are not chasing them
you are chasing the part of you that awakens in their presence
and the journey is not toward them
but through you

When you remember them
you remember yourself

Integration

- What did I feel the moment I met the one who mirrored my soul?

- What truths have been revealed through this connection about love, about myself, about union?

- What parts of me have been activated, and what parts have been challenged or undone?

- In what ways has this relationship been a catalyst for my awakening and remembrance?

- Am I willing to see this love as a divine reflection, not a destination?

I honour the one who reflected my light and my shadow
The one who stirred what I had buried
The one who called my soul home
I do not chase
I remember
And in remembering, I return to the truth that love was never outside of me, it was always within

Chapter Six

Starseed Origins & Celestial Homes: Remembering Where We Come From

Returning to the knowing of our galactic families, soul lineages, and the feeling of belonging beyond Earth

You always knew
not with your mind
but in the quiet
in the stars
in the ache for something you couldn't name

Earth was never all of it
you looked up and felt the echo
you stood in silence and something ancient stirred
something that didn't begin here
and hasn't ended

You are not from one place
you are a soul that has lived in many systems
held by light that doesn't burn
guided by beings that don't speak but remember
you completely

Pleiadian
Sirian
Lyran
and others you don't yet have words for
you've sat in star councils
moved through gateways
whispered light codes before you had a voice

Your longing is not confusion
it is orientation
it is your compass recalibrating to a frequency
you've always carried

Your sensitivity
your wisdom

your loneliness
your resistance to systems that make no sense
these are not flaws
they are clues
markers of your origin

You are a bridge
a translator
a soul seeded here to anchor what Earth forgot

You do not need to remember the names
only the feeling
only the truth that pulses beneath the skin when
you hear
you are not alone
you never were

This is not imagination
it is memory
returning

Integration

- When did I first feel that Earth was not my only home?

- What inner sensations or dreams have pointed to origins beyond this planet?

- How does it feel to acknowledge that I carry codes from other star systems?

- What gifts or sensitivities might be connected to my soul lineage?

- In what ways am I here to serve as a bridge between realms?

I honour the knowing that cannot be explained
The longing that leads me home
The memories that arrive as feelings, not facts
I welcome the parts of me that stretch across galaxies
I remember that I came here not to belong to Earth but to bring something to it

Chapter Seven

Soul Alchemy: Chaos, Purging & Integration

When the soul burns away illusion through fire, shadow, and light, bringing all parts home to the centre

This is the part they don't always speak of
the part after the light
after the meeting
after the remembrance

The fire doesn't come first
the fire comes when the truth has arrived
and everything false must fall

You purge not because you are broken
but because you are being remade

The illusions you lived inside, about love, about self,
about safety, begin to crack
the roles dissolve
the patterns unravel
and what's left is raw
real
unfiltered soul

You grieve things you thought you healed
you rage
you isolate
you dig through lifetimes of silence
just to find a voice you can trust

It is chaotic
it is holy
it is uncomfortable
it is divine

This is the alchemy
not pretty

not poetic
but honest

You burn
you question everything
you wonder if you imagined all of it
but even in your lowest moment
you are being purified

Not punished
purified

What no longer aligns is pulled from your field
what cannot go forward dissolves
what is true will remain
and what is true
is you

You are not being undone
you are being returned

This is the soul in flame
and what emerges from this
is not who you were
but who you've always been

Integration

- What has been burned away in me that I once thought I needed?

- Where have I resisted the fire, and where have I surrendered to it?

- What emotional patterns, beliefs, or attachments have surfaced for release?

- How have chaos and discomfort served as portals to deeper truth?

- Am I willing to trust the fire as an ally, not a threat?

I honour the fire that stripped me bare
The chaos that revealed my core
The shadows that showed me what was still unloved
I do not fear the unraveling
I trust the alchemy
I am not becoming someone new
I am returning to the one I've always been

Chapter Eight

Embodiment: Becoming the Living Light

The integration of remembrance into form, living as soul, speaking as truth, walking as love

This is not the moment you ascend
This is the moment you arrive

Fully
present
human
holy

The journey inward does not end in the stars
it returns to your breath
to your skin
to your voice
to the small moments that become sacred because
you are now inside them

You are no longer chasing alignment
you are living it

Not in perfection
but in presence

You speak slower
you listen more
you honour the body as temple
you treat time as ceremony

Embodiment is not the absence of emotion
it is the fullness of feeling
without collapse
without denial

You say yes only when your soul does
you say no without guilt

you soften without breaking
you stand without hardening

This is remembrance in motion
this is light in human form
this is you, becoming the living bridge between
what was, and what is

You are not performing love
you are radiating it
without trying
without effort
because it is no longer something you do
it is who you are

Integration

- What does it mean to me to live as a soul, not just know I have one?

- In what areas of my life have I already begun to embody truth?

- What habits or expressions no longer reflect who I've become?

- How can I honour my body, my voice, and my choices as sacred vessels of light?

- What does it feel like to live as love, not just seek it?

I do not chase the light
I am the light
I live it
Speak it
Breathe it
I do not have to leave this body to return to truth
I carry it in my hands
In my steps
In the quiet choices no one sees
I am the soul embodied
And I am home

Chapter Nine

The Return: Wholeness, Remembrance & Homecoming

The soul's quiet landing into itself, no longer seeking, no longer waiting, just being fully home

You thought the journey was outward
that you had to reach something
find someone
unlock a secret

But the truth was never far
it was always within
beneath the noise
behind the longing
inside the ache

You do not arrive
you remember

Slowly
softly
you settle into yourself

You no longer chase light
you embody it
you no longer search for signs
you become the knowing

Home is not a place
not a person
not a moment in time
it is the stillness of your soul remembering itself

You stop waiting
you stop proving
you stop asking if you are enough

Because you are no longer divided
no longer fragmented
no longer forgetting

This is the return
the return to presence
the return to peace
the return to you

And nothing is missing
nothing ever was

Integration

- What have I stopped chasing because I now know it lives within me?

- How has my definition of home changed throughout this journey?

- In what moments do I feel most whole, most present, most me?

- What does it feel like to no longer seek, but simply be?

- Can I trust that I am already home?

I *do not need to arrive*
I am already here
I am not a question seeking an answer
I am a soul resting in its own knowing
I do not return to who I was
I return to who I've always been
And here
in this breath
I am home

you were never lost
you were never broken
you were simply remembering

not in a straight line
not in the way they told you
but in fragments
in feelings
in fire
in love

you do not need to become
you are
you do not need to seek
you carry it all

the soul remembers
always

About the Author

blanche johanna is a spiritual author, channel, and keeper of soulstream transmissions devoted to remembrance, union, and return.

Her work lives beyond genre, woven from codes of light, lived experience, and divine memory. Each creation is an offering, a portal, a mirror.

Through books, oracle decks, and embodied offerings, she supports Twin Flames, starseeds, and awakening souls in reconnecting with their original essence.

The Soul Remembers is her second body of work, a living transmission for those walking the path of deep remembering.

www.blanchejohanna.com

www.ingramcontent.com/pod-product-compliance
Lightning Source LLC
Chambersburg PA
CBHW040732220426
43209CB00087B/1599